Musical Instruments

Percussion

Revised and updated

Wendy Lynch

Heinemann
LIBRARY

www.heinemann.co.uk/library
Visit our website to find out more information about **Heinemann Library** books.

To order:
☎ Phone ++44 (0)1865 888066
🖹 Send a fax to ++44 (0)1865 314091
🖥 Visit the Heinemann Bookshop at www.heinemann.co.uk/library to browse our catalogue and order online.

First published in Great Britain by Heinemann Library,
Halley Court, Jordan Hill,
Oxford OX2 8EJ, part of Harcourt Education.
Heinemann is a registered trademark of Harcourt
Education Ltd.

Editorial: Clare Lewis and Audrey Stokes
Design: Joanna Hinton-Malivoire and John Walker
Picture research: Erica Newbery
Production: Helen McCreath

Origination: Modern Age Repro House Ltd.
Printed and bound in China by South
China Printing Co. Ltd.

10-digit ISBN 0-431-12917-7
13-digit ISBN 978-0-431-12917-4

10 09 08 07 06
10 9 8 7 6 5 4 3 2 1

British Library Cataloguing in Publication Data
Lynch, Wendy
Percussion. – (Musical Instruments) - 2nd ed.
1. Percussion instruments – Juvenile literature
I. Title
786.8
A full catalogue record for this book is available from
the British Library.

Acknowledgements
The publishers would like to thank the following for
permission to reproduce photographs: Gareth Boden,
pp. 16, 24, 28, 29; Lebrecht collection, pp. 11 (G
Salter), 14 (Chris Stock), 19 (Chris Stock); Magnum
(Ian Berry), p. 22; Photodisc, pp. 6, 7, 12; Photo edit, p.
17 (Spencer Grant), p. 21 (Michael Newman); Pictor,
pp. 4, 15, 20; Redferns, pp. 8 (Andrew Lepley), 26 (Leon
Morris), 27 (Mick Hutson); Rex Features pp. 5, 13 (J.
Lingo), 25 (Maria Antonelli); Robert Harding, p. 23;
Sally Greenhill, p. 18; Travel Ink (David Toase), p. 9.

Cover photograph reproduced with permission of
Alamy Images/ Brand X Pictures.

The publishers would like to thank Nancy Harris for
her assistance in the preparation of this book.

Every effort has been made to contact copyright
holders of any material reproduced in this book. Any
omissions will be rectified in subsequent printings if
notice is given to the publishers.

The paper used to print this book comes from
sustainable resources.

Any words appearing in the text in bold, **like this**, are explained in the Glossary.

Contents

Making music together

There are many musical instruments in the world. Each instrument makes a different sound. We can make music together by playing these instruments in a band or an **orchestra.** An orchestra is a large group of musicians.

Bands and orchestras are made up of different groups of instruments. One of these groups is called percussion. Above is a steel band. Everyone in the band is playing a percussion instrument.

What are percussion instruments?

Here you can see many different percussion instruments. They all make very different sounds. Drums beat. Cymbals crash. Tambourines jingle.

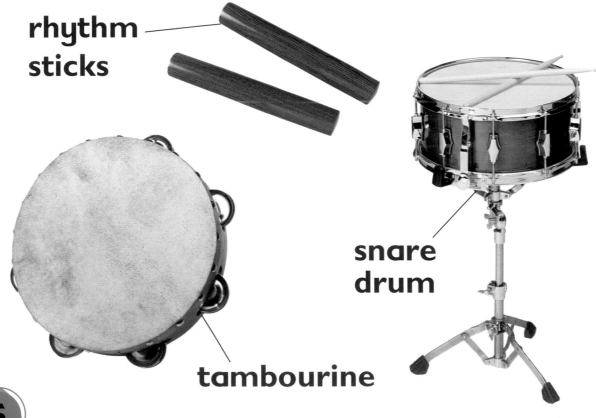

rhythm sticks

snare drum

tambourine

You bang, shake, or scrape percussion instruments to make a sound. They are made of strong materials. They are made of gold and steel. They are made of bronze and wood.

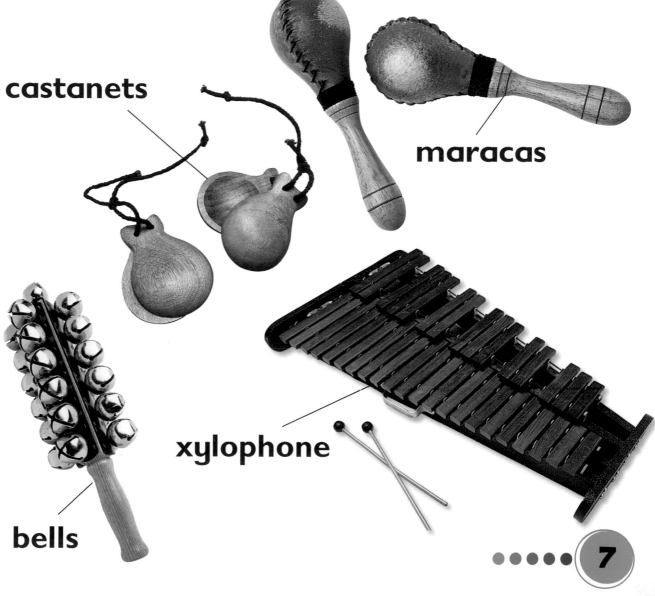

castanets

maracas

xylophone

bells

The drum

These are bongo drums. You tap them with your fingers or with your hands. You can make patterns of long or short sounds. This pattern is called a **rhythm**.

You can play the drum with other instruments. You can play it in a band or an **orchestra**. The drums play the rhythm for the other instruments.

How the sound is made

You hit the top of the drum to make a sound. This makes the air inside the drum move up and down. This movement is called **vibration**. When air vibrates, it makes a sound.

This is a cymbal. You crash the two
metal discs together to make a sound.
It makes the metal **vibrate**.

Making a noise

The top of the drum is called the head. It is made of skin or plastic. Some drums make the same sound all the time. You can change the sound in others.

A sound can be high or low. This is called **pitch**. You press a pedal to change pitch for some drums. You **tighten** screws to change pitch for others.

Types of drum

The **snare drum** has wires under the skin. They rattle when you hit the drum.

oil drum

You make steel drums from oil drums.
You hit the top in different places to
change the sound. They sound very
different from other drums.

Triangle and xylophone

This is a triangle. You tap the triangle with a beater to make a high, tinkling sound. The note you play on the triangle is always the same.

The xylophone has wooden bars. Each bar makes a different sound. These ring when you tap them with a beater. Some xylophones have a **hollow** wooden sound box under the bars.

Percussion section

In school you may play some other
percussion instruments. You may
play the chimes. You may play the
tambourine or the **rhythm** sticks.

Some percussion instruments are untuned. This means that they make the same sound all the time. A triangle is untuned.

Other percussion instruments are tuned. Tubular bells are tuned. They make different sounds.

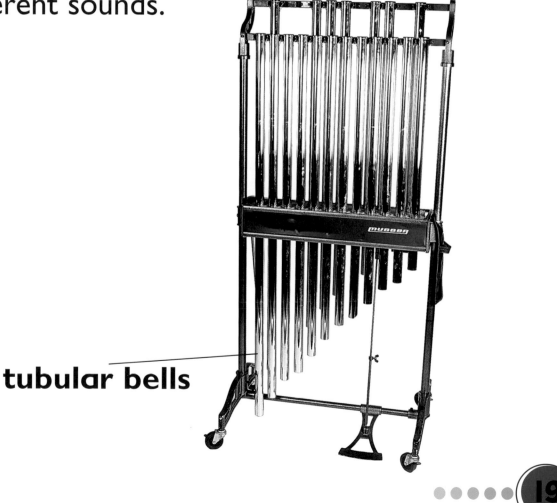

tubular bells

The wider family

Castanets are two pieces of wood tied on a cord. You click the wood together to make a sound. Castanets are used in Spain to make a **rhythm** for Spanish dancing.

The tambourine has small metal discs in its side. You hold the tambourine in your hand. When you shake the tambourine, you can hear the discs jingle.

Around the world

The kalungu is from Africa. It is called the talking drum. You can hear this drum across long distances. You can hear it across forests.

The bonang is a set of gongs. It comes from Indonesia. You can hear the bonang in a **gamelan orchestra**. A gamelan orchestra is an orchestra you can hear in Indonesia.

Famous musicians and composers

Haydn was a famous **composer**. He wrote the Surprise Symphony. The surprise comes when you hear a very loud beat of a drum.

Evelyn Glennie is a famous percussionist.
Evelyn is deaf. She can feel the
vibration of the music as she plays.

New music

You can hear percussion instruments in **jazz** and **rock bands** today. The drum kit is important in **pop music**. It plays the beat. This helps people to dance in time to the music.

You can also make the sound of a
drum with an electronic drum kit. You
hit the pad of the drum. This sends a
pulse to a control unit. This control
unit makes the sound of the drum.

Sound activity

- You can make your own percussion instruments.

- Put some rice in a plastic cup.

- Put another plastic cup on top of it and tape them together.

- Shake your shaker!

- You can make a xylophone.

- Put six bottles or glasses in a line.

- Put different amounts of water in each bottle.

- Tap the bottles with a stick or wooden spoon.

Thinking about percussion

You can find the answers to all of these questions in this book.

1. How do you play percussion instruments?
2. Which drum plays the lowest, loudest notes?
3. What is the difference between a tuned and untuned percussion instrument?
4. What is a kalungu?

More books to read

Little Nippers: Making Music: Banging, Angela Aylmore (Heinemann Library, 2005)

Little Nippers: Making Music: Shaking, Angela Aylmore (Heinemann Library, 2005)

Musical Instruments of the World: Percussion, M. J. Knight (Franklin Watts Ltd, 2005)

Glossary

composer person who writes new music

gamelan orchestra orchestra you can hear in Indonesia

hollow empty inside

jazz old style of music from the United States that is often made up as it is played

orchestra large group of musicians who play their musical instruments together
You say *or-kes-tra*

pitch the highness or lowness of a sound or musical note

pop music music of the last 50 years. A lot of people like this music.

pulse single beat

rhythm repeated beats or sounds that make a pattern
You say *rith-um*

rock bands group of musicians who play a kind of pop music with a strong beat

snare drum drum with strings or wires stretched across it

tighten to make something tighter or more close fitting

vibrate move up or down or from side to side very quickly